101 Coolest Things to Do in Peru

Introduction

So you're going to Peru, huh? You lucky lucky thing! You are sure in for a treat because Peru is one of the most dynamic and exciting countries on the face of the earth. There's a mix of incredible landscapes, ancient ruins, world-class food, and well curated museums that makes Peru one of the most enduringly popular tourist destinations on the face of the earth.

In this guide, we'll be giving you the low down on:
- the very best things to shove in your pie hole, whether that's traditional street eats from Peruvian alleyways, or plates of roasted guinea pig
- the best shopping so that you can take a little piece of London back home with you, whether that's from traditional weavers in the mountains, or from Pisco distilleries
- the most thrilling outdoor activities, such as trekking the Inca Trail, or even riding a buggy over undulating sand dunes
- the coolest historical and cultural sights that you simply cannot afford to miss like ancient Inca Ruins and contemporary art museums
- where to party like someone a true Peruvian and get down with the locals
- and tonnes more coolness besides!

Let's not waste any more time – here are the 101 coolest things not to miss in Peru!

1. Check out the Palacio de Gobierno in Lima

The capital of Peru, Lima, is a city with no shortage of beautiful architecture, but our favourite building in the whole of the city might just be the Palacia de Gobierno. This building is the official residence of the President of Peru, and was constructed in 1535 but has undergone many renovations since. There is a changing of the guard every day at noon outside the Palace, which is free to watch.

2. Visit the Floating Islands of the Uru People

Any highlight to visiting Lake Titicaca has to be a trip to the floating Uros Islands of the Uru people. The islands are not natural, but constructed entirely from the totora reeds that grow all around and are extremely buoyant. It's a great idea to take an organised tour of the islands via boat, because this way you can explore many of them and get to know their history and culture. You can even stay the night on a reed boat if you wish.

3. See the Terraced Ruins of Moray

A little off the beaten track and around 50km outside of Cusco, you can find the very unique ruins of Moray. Here you will find deep bowl shaped hollows with terraces that climb up to the valley floor, making the whole thing look rather like a Roman amphitheatre. The use of these terraces is not completely known, but it is thought that the Incas used them as an agricultural laboratory with different micro-climates at different levels of the terraces.

4. Get Close to Alligators at Fundo Pedrito

If you love the idea of getting back to nature, a trip to the port city of Iquitos is an absolute must. This tourist town is the gateway to much of the northern jungle and tribal villages. One of the places that you can visit nearby is called Fundo Pedrito, a fish farm that's located in the middle of the jungle. You can feed the fish there, but most visitors go for one reason – the alligators. There are many of them in the lake, and it's truly incredible to see the gators interacting and living as they would in their natural habitat.

5. Trek Through the Mountains to Machu Picchu

Going on the Inca Trail and seeing the majestic Machu Picchu is such an obvious thing to suggest for Peru that we almost didn't include it in this guide of cool things, but somehow leaving it out did not feel right at all. If you're going to splash out once on your trip to Peru, make sure that it's on finding a great tour provider who'll make your Inca Trail experience one to always remember. A four to five day winding hike will allow you to fully explore this part of the world where the Andes mountains meet the Amazon rainforest. Your hike should end with a stunning view of Machu Picchu, a 15th century citadel and the most familiar icon of the Inca civilisation.

6. Enjoy the Deliciousness of Peruvian Tamales

Tamales are a mainstay of Latin American cuisine, but each country makes their tamales slightly differently. These are typically eaten at Christmas time, but let's face it, there is no bad time to eat a tamal, and they make for a filling breakfast that will surely see you through to lunchtime. As with other tamales, Peruvian tamales are typically made with a masa dough with some kind of steamed meat mixture inside, but the difference in Peru is that Pisco, the national drink, is thrown into the sauce to give it a unique kick.

7. Indulge a Wine Lover at the Tacama Vineyard

There are places in South America that are very well known for their incredible wines, but if you are a wine lover, you might have a stronger urge to visit Argentina or Chile. While the Peruvian wine scene is not quite as well established, this is certainly not to say that there are not some fabulous pockets of wine culture in Peru. In fact, Tacama Vineyard is the oldest vineyard in all of South America. There are guided tours in both Spanish and English on the premises so that you can really get to grips with the local wine culture.

8. Say Hi to the Animals at Parque de las Leyendas

If you are travelling with kids to Peru, something that you can do to keep them entertained is go on a trip to the zoo at Parque de la Leyendas in Lima. The zoo has separate areas for the coast, jungle and highlands, and you can explore many different animals native to Peru throughout these zones. There's also a baby zoo, where kids can really get up close to the animals, pet them, and feed them.

9. Be Wowed by an Illuminated Water Fountain Show

Because Lima is a capital city, there are times when it can be crowded and busy. One great place to escape the hustle and the bustle is the Parque de la Reserva. But there is something other than the ample amounts of green space that makes us really love this park, and that's the light and water show that takes place every between Wednesday and Sunday every week. All the fountains become illuminated with bright colours and lasers.

10. Get to Grips With the Ins and Outs of Peruvian Gastronomy

Of course, one of the best ways to understand a culture is to understand its food. There's no shortage of deliciousness to eat when you're in Peru, but to understand more about the local cuisines, a trip to the Peruvian Gastronomy Museum in Lima is definitely recommended. This museum will lead you on a journey through 2000 years of culinary history. The highlight has to be a room decorated to Pisco, the national spirit of Peru.

11. Go Trout Fishing in the Peruvian Andes

If your idea of a perfect getaway is to sit on the edge of a river with a fishing rod in your hand to try and catch a bite, Peru is a country where you can enjoy some of the very best fishing in Latin America. The place to be for trout fishing is the upper Urubamba river in the Andes, which as well as hosting a large trout population, is absolutely beautiful. You'll also find some native fish species such as karachi and suche.

12. Discover pre-Columbian art at the Larco Museum

Larco Museum in Lima is an incredible place, housed in a colonial mansion, and full of incomparable treasures. Inside, you can find more than 3000 items, with things like ceramics, textiles, and precious metal artefacts from ore-Columbian Peru. Something very unique about this museum is that there's a room dedicated to erotic archaeology, with items like ceramic pots showing sexual positions, many of which were destroyed by the Spanish conquerors.

13. Try a Local Cusco Beer, Supay Quinoa Pale Ale

When you think of beer loving nations around the world, places like Belgium or Germany would probably first spring to mind, but you absolutely shouldn't underestimate Peru when it comes to beer loving. One of the more unique beers we tried in the country can be found in Cusco, and it's called the Supay Quinoa Pale Ale. This beer is brewed locally, is only available in Cusco, and since it's made with quinoa it's possible for people with gluten free diets to drink it.

14. Explore the Deepest Canyon in the World, Cotahuasi Canyon

For outdoor adventurers, we think there's one spot in Peru that you simply cannot miss, the Cotahuasi Canyon, which happens to be the deepest canyon in the whole world, with twice the depth of the Grand Canyon. The deepest parts of the ravine are only accessible to the most experienced of river runners, but the whole terrain of the canyon is wonderful for hiking and simply being outdoors.

15. Learn Something at the Museum of Royal Tombs of Sipan

The Royal Tombs Museum in Lambayeque is often thought of as one of the most impressive archaeological museums in South America, and when you enter you will understand why. The museum has an unusual pyramid shaped exterior, replicating that of a Moche tomb, and inside you can find many artefacts from the Moche civilisation who lived in Peru from the 1st to the 8th centuries. You can find gold and silver artefacts, jewellery, precious stones, headdresses, and more besides.

16. Enjoy a Cocktail With a View in Lima

Lima is a very beautiful city, but you can only appreciate the true extent of its grandeur if you take in the city from a great height, and what better way of doing that by drinking a sunset cocktail on a rooftop bar? The Souk Bar at the Radisson Hotel is the perfect place to do exactly that. The souk atmosphere may not feel all that Peruvian, but with a Pisco Sour in your hand and a view over Lima, there should be no mistaking exactly where you are.

17. Shop for Peruvian Souvenirs at Feria Artesanal

As a capital city, there's no shortage of great places to go for some shopping in Lima, but with so much choice you might just feel overwhelmed and unsure of where to do your souvenir shopping. If you just have one morning or afternoon to grab everything you need to take home with you, the Feria Artesanal, and artisanal market, is the place to go. You'll mostly find local prices here and an assortment of locally made, authentic items.

18. Feel the Force of Ancient History at Huaca Pucllana

Peru is the ultimate travel destination for history buffs, and there are ruins to be found all over the country. But if you are in Lima, and you don't feel like trekking outside of the city, there are some awesome ruins in the Miraflores district called Huaca Pucllana. This is an adobe ceremonial centre that dates all the way back to 500AD. We recommend visiting at night when the ruins are beautifully illuminated. And there's even a restaurant there where you can eat your dinner.

19. Fill Your Stomach with a Butifarra

When you are at the point of collapsing from hunger in Peru, a delicious Butifarra sandwich is certain to bring you all the way back to life. This traditional sandwich consists of fluffy bread rolls filled with jamon del pais (roasted ham that is seasoned with garlic, chilli, and spices) and a sweet onion salsa. These are totally moreish so we wouldn't be surprised if you came back for seconds.

20. Have a Camping Adventure in Lomas de Lachay

Peru is a nature lover's paradise, and you can find national parks dotted all over the country. Lomas de Lachay is a national reserve that you can find just 105km north of the capital city, Lima. There are undulating hills and beautiful greenery all around that make this park a wonderful place to hike, and if you really want to get away from it all, you'll be pleased to know that there is also a campground inside the park where you can stay the night and hear nothing but the sounds of chirping birds in the morning.

21. Pay a Visit to the Oldest Pisco Distillery in Peru

A trip to Peru would not be complete without sipping on pisco, the national spirit of the country. Pisco is a spirit made from distilling grape wine so it becomes a brandy, and you can learn all about it at Peru's first ever pisco distillery, Pisco Porton. This very special place is nestled in the valley of the Ica winemaking region, and it was established all the way back in 1684. Why not visit and try the good stuff yourself?

22. Try Parasailing From Lima's Malecon

If you fancy yourself as something of an adventurer, you may think that you need to disappear into the mountains or the jungle to have a thrill seeking experience, but that is actually far from the case. In Lima, there is the opportunity to have a parasailing adventure from the picturesque Malecon. Gliders jump off the cliffs and hover in the air before hitting the ocean below.

23. Join in With the Festivities of Puno Week

Outside of Peru, Puno week is virtually unheard of, but inside the country, it's one of the most important celebrations of the year since it commemorates the life of the first Inca, Manco Capac. The celebrations happen in the first week of November, and Puno Day, the major day of the celebrations, is November 5th. The place to be for the celebrations is, of course, Puno, and there's lots of music, dancing, eating, drinking, and merriment.

24. Enjoy a Boat Tour of the Palomino Islands

When people think of Peru, they often first think of mountains and ruins, and neglect to even realise that there's an expanse of coastline in Peru as well. There are even islands off the coast, and if you are a water baby, you'll love the opportunity to tour the Palomino Islands which lie just off the coast of Lima. One of the highlights of these boat tours is getting to see the 8000 sea lions that live off the Palomino Islands up close.

25. Visit the Largest Clothing and Textile Market in Latin America

To really get to know a city, you have to become acquainted with its market culture, and there's quite a few impressive markets across Lima. For us, the coolest market of all is not a food market but a textile and fabrics market called Gamarra, which is actually the largest textile market in all of Latin America. It takes up 24 blocks and you can find 20,000 textiles shops there! So if you want some tailored clothing while in Peru, you know exactly where to go.

26. Chow Down on Cow Hearts on a Stick

If your idea of a great holiday is to spend all your time trying new and exotic foods, you're certainly in luck in Peru. Something that you probably wouldn't have tried before is called Anticuchos, and these are essentially cows' hearts that are grilled on a stick. Peruvians love spice and flavour, and so you'll often find them marinated in garlic, cumin and vinegar.

These are a popular street food meal, so don't be scared to chow down in the open air.

27. Go White Water Rafting on the Canete River

If you have something of an adventurous spirit, you'll be more than satisfied in Peru, where you can have all sorts of adventurous activities, and one of the most enduring popular of these has to be white water rafting on the Canete River, which has Class V rapids. If you don't know what that means, just know that this river is hella powerful. This experience probably isn't for white water rafting first timers!

28. Enjoy a Traditional Plate of Causa Rellena

Causa Rellena is not a Peruvian dish that you here much about outside of Peru, but most travellers who go to the country and try it end up totally falling in love with it. The idea of a causa rellena is really quite simple. There are two layers of baked mashed potato that are filled with some kind of filling between. Because mashed potato is dense, the filling is usually something lighter like chicken salad or seafood salad. This is a wonderful light lunch, Peruvian style.

29. Celebrate Carnaval in Cajamarca

Carnaval is a festivity that's full of Latin spirit, but most people would associate it with Brazil and Rio de Janeiro. Actually, there's an incredible Carnaval culture in Peru as well, and specifically in the small city of Cajamarca in the north of the country. The celebrations last for almost a month but are at their most vibrant in the first half of February. Some of the activities during this time include a beauty pageant, a decorated cars contest, a traditional dance around trees, and lots of music, dancing, eating and drinking in general.

30. Be Stunned by a Mohican Tomb Complex

Peru is a country that has so much history to explore, and one of our favourite spots for exploring Peru in ancient times is Huaca Rajada, a Mohican tomb complex dating to around 300 AD. This complex was originally built as the political and religious centre of the region, and then transformed into a tomb complex for important burials. The most famous tomb of all is of the Lord of Sipan, which was found in very good condition and totally untouched by thieves.

31. Ride the Waves of Puerto Chicama

When you think of surfing destinations around the world, the coastlines of Hawaii or California might be the first places that spring to mind, but if you are really serious about surfing, Peru also offers some spectacular waves. We reckon that Puerto Chicama, a surfing town in north-western Peru might just be the place for riding waves in the country. Even if you've never tried surfing before, there are some local schools that can help you out.

32. Indulge a Sweet Tooth With Mazamorra Morada

Peru is better known for its savoury dishes than sweet treats, but if you do have a sweet tooth, we don't think that you'll be disappointed on your trip to the country. Something dessert lovers should look out for is Mazamorra Morada, which is made from a purple corn found in the country. Chopped apple and quince is added to the water of this corn to create a unique kind of jelly, and this is often served up with rice pudding.

33. Keep the Kids Entertained at Parque de la Imaginacion

If you are travelling with kids, you surely want to give them memories that last a lifetime, but travelling with children can also be a huge challenge. When you're in Lima, take them to the Parque de la Imaginacion and they are sure to be entertained. This place is also known as the Science Centre, and there are tonnes of interactive features that will keep restless kids happy. Inside, you can learn the science behind things like aviation, earthquakes, and firefighting.

34. Start Your Day With Caldo de Gallina from San Pedro Market

While you are in the charming city of Cusco, you'll find that there is one dish that is more present than any other, and that's a warming bowl of Caldo de Gallina, Peru's answer to your granny's chicken noodle soup. Although you can find this soup in virtually every local eatery, we like the stalls at the San Pedro Market for their rustic charm and generous portions. This simple chicken soup has meat, root veggies, broth, and sometimes pasta, and it's very popular for breakfast time to combat the Cusco chill.

35. Discover Contemporary Art in Lima

We all know that Peru is a country with lots of history and a great cultural heritage, but what of the contemporary arts culture in Peru? Well, arts lovers will be glad to know that it's alive and well, and you can discover the very best of it on a trip to Museo Mario Testino, set up by the Italian fashion photographer himself. Inside you'll find contemporary art exhibitions, art performances, talks, and even workshops to learn a new creative skill.

36. Enjoy World Music at the Festival de Los 7 Mares

If you are a huge music fan, you need to know about the Festival de Los 7 Mares (translated as Festival of the 7 Seas) because it's at this festival that you can experience incredible world music from every corner of the planet. The festival is hosted every year in Exposition Park in Lima. Whether you would like to hear traditional Peruvian music, rock out to European guitar bands, or listen to music from Asia, there will be something for you.

37. Start Your Day With a Cup of Coca Tea

The coca leaf, which is something that is used to be make the drug cocaine, is illegal in most parts of the world, but not in Peru, and particularly in Cusco where products made from the Coca leaf abound. Cusco has a higher elevation that most other places in Peru, and before starting on the Inca Trail or one of the other treks, it's a good idea to bed down for a few days and get acclimatised to the altitude. Coca tea is something that can help with this, so why not give it a try?

38. Have a Deep Sea Fishing Adventure in Tumbes

Although Peru is best known for its mountainous landscapes, there's also some awesome coastline, and just off the coast of a town called Tumbes there is incredible deep sea fishing. If you enjoy fishing, there are many companies there that can take you out on the water to secure a big catch. In those waters you can find fish such as black marlin, striped marlin, roosterfish, swordfish, tuna, amberjack, and more besides.

39. Shop for Souvenirs at San Blas Market

Before you leave beautiful Peru, you will certainly want to go shopping for some traditional items so that you can always have a piece of Peru with you. In our opinion, the best place for souvenir shopping in Cusco is the San Blas Market, which is a popular shopping and eating hub for locals and tourists alike. You can find anything from antique blankets to fine jewellery, ceramics to wood carvings, and just about everything in between.

40. Discover Peruvian Art at Pinacoteca Municipal Ignacio Merino

If you find yourself in Lima on a drizzly day, fear not because there's enough museums in the capital to shelter you from the rain for days on end. For arts lovers, we are particularly enamoured by Pinacoteca Municipal Ignacio Merino, which houses one of the most important collections of Peruvian art in the country. Inside, you can find around 600 works from the 19th and 20th centuries, and many important Peruvian painters such as Pancho Fierro and Jose Sabogal are on display.

41. Take a Tour of the Ballestas Islands

If you want to get away from the tourist mayhem of Peru and visit some places that are not quite so frequented by the tourist crowd, a trip to the coastal area can be a great idea, and a boat trip to the Ballestas Islands even better. These islands have many dramatic arches and caves, which are great to explore. There's also an abundance of sea lions living there that you'll be able to see up close.

42. Understand the History of Slavery in Peru

While Peru is certainly a very beautiful country, there is absolutely no denying that there is a dark side to Peru's history as well, and you can learn about the history of slavery in Peru at the Afro-Peruvian Museum in Lima. The museum explains the history of Afro-Americans in Peru, with a strong emphasis on the lives of slaves. You'll also learn about the way African culture made its imprint on the Peruvian identity.

43. Feed Manatee Babies at the Amazonian Manatee Orphanage

One of the highlights of visiting Peru is that you will have the opportunity to get up close to animals that you would never encounter at home, and sometimes rare species such as the Amazonian Manatee. Located in Iquitos, the Amazonian Manatee Orphanage is a place that looks after the most adorable baby manatees, also known as sea cows. Something really special about this place is that you can actually feed the baby animals, which is sure to be an experience you'll never forget.

44. Have a Mind Altering Experience With Ayuhasca

Ayuhasca is a natural drug that is found in the Peruvian jungle, and it has recently grown in popularity with Western tourists thanks to its hallucinogenic and mind altering properties that for some people have been totally life changing. This is an ancient, pre-Hispanic drug, and taking the drug involves taking part in a whole ceremony with a shaman that can be up to two weeks long. Some people who have experienced this have reported feelings of immense calm in the months to calm after the ceremony. Just be sure to do your research about reputable centres before signing up.

45. Have a Day of Learning at the Museum of Natural History

Located in Lima and open since 1918, the Natural History Museum in Peru is full of fascinating items. If you have a kid who is interested in the natural world, this would be a wonderful place to take them. Inside, you'll find items that date all the way back to the Stone Age, and some of the highlights include the fossilised skeleton of a sperm whale, and the fossils of glacial animals.

46. Get Spooked by Mummies at Museo Leymebamba

Back in 1997, more than 200 mummies and their burial offerings were excavated from the Leymebamba area of Peru, and now you have the chance to see all of the exceptional findings at the Museo Leymebamba. While the mummies are definitely the reason why people visit this museum, we think that the building itself, which has been built using local and traditional techniques, is also very impressive. Plus it has an incredible orchid garden, with over 100 orchid species.

47. Explore the Floating Village of Belen

Belen is one of the most unique places on this planet. It lies at the edge of Iquitos city, which is the largest city in the world (with a population of 400,000) that cannot be reached by road. Belen is its own floating neighbourhood market, and it's a must visit if you really want to get to grips with local life off the beaten track in Peru. At the market, you'll find all kinds of Amazonian products to buy, such as tropical river fish, turtles, frogs, monkeys, herbal medicines, and more besides.

48. Peruse pre-Columbian Ceramics at Museo de Arte de Lima

Commonly known as MALI, the Museum of Art of Lima is a must visit for all art fanatics in the city. This is the one museum in all of the country that has the most Peruvian art, right from ancient times and up to the present day. We think that the pre-Columbian art and objects are especially impressive, with items that date all the way back to 1200BC. Entry is cheaper on Sundays.

49. Have a Wild Dune Buggy Ride in Huacachina

Huacachina is a unique village in the southwest of the country that is totally surrounded by undulating sand dunes. This landscape is very beautiful but you can do more than just look at it as you can even take dune buggy rides over the sand. These dune buggies do not offer a relaxed car ride, so you should be prepared to get thrown around a bit. But if you're an adventurer, it's something you will want to do over and over again.

50. Eat at Food Stalls at the Mercado Central in Lima

While it's true that Lima is a first-rate foodie destination, to get the true local experience, you should steer clear of the city's fancy restaurants for at least a few of your meals. The Mercado Central is a bustling hub of market eateries where you'll have plenty of choice, and you can eat shoulder to shoulder with the local people. You can find all kinds of local eats there, including cheap as chips ceviche.

51. Be Wowed by the Gocta Waterfall

There is nothing quite like the sight of a cascading waterfall to make you feel connected to nature. Well, Peru has its fair share of impressive waterfalls, but we are particularly enamoured by Gocta Waterfall, which can be found in the province of Chachapoyas in the Amazon. The waterfall is 771 metres in height, which makes it one of the tallest waterfalls in the world, and you can even swim in the pool at the bottom even if it takes 3 hours to hike there.

52. Look at Objects From Peru's Ancient Civilisations

Hans Bruning was a German researcher and archaeologist who spent much of his adult life in Peru, and the Bruning Museum in Lambayeque is based on his impressive collections. Today, the Bruning Museum contains more than 1500 artefacts from the various cultures of northern Peru, such as the Moche, Chimu, and Vicus civilisations. There's not much written information inside the museum, so it can be a great idea to take one of the English tours.

53. Learn About Afro-Peruvian Slavery at Casa Hacienda San Jose

Chincha, which lies around 200km south of Lima, is the heart of Afro-Peruvian culture in Peru, and the people here are fiercely proud of their mixed heritage, and the struggle through slavery. One place where you can really feel this history is at Casa Hacienda San Jose, a hacienda that once had 1000 slaves. Once inside, a highlight is exploring the network of tunnels underneath the building, linking it to five other haciendas and the port.

54. Chow Down on Guinea Pig in Cusco

In Peru, you can sample all kinds of weird and wonderful foods, and to a Western sensibility, guinea pig must be one of the weirdest of them all. You might think that guinea pig is something that people eat when they can't afford other types of meat, but this is far from the case. Guinea pig is a delicacy in Peru, and it's reserved for special occasions like birthdays. It's particularly popular in Cusco, and we think it tastes like a cross between the dark meat of chicken and duck. Would you dare?

55. Go Bird Watching in Manu National Park

Manu National Park is no ordinarily place. It is a veritable paradise with 1.5 million hectares of open land, which ranges from 150 metres to 4200 metres above sea level. With so much diversity, Manu National Park is one of the best spots for bird watching in the whole world. In fact, there's over 1000 bird species registered there, and this makes up around 10% of all the types of birds in the world. You'll find gulls, sandpipers, kingfishers, and loads more types.

56. Sip on Craft Beers in the Sacred Valley

If you enjoy a drink or two, you might expect to be sipping on Pisco Sours day and night in Peru. And while there is certainly nothing wrong with a Pisco Sour, beer fans aren't left out in the cold either. The Sacred Valley region of Cusco has its own microbrewery called Cerveceria del Valle Sagrado that is producing beers right on the land of Peru and only supplying to local bars. You can, however, arrange with the brewery to have your very own tasting sessions.

57. Take the Alternative Salkantey Trek to Machu Picchu

If you want to see Machu Picchu, and of course you do, you might think that you have to take the Inca Trail. Not the case. If the Inca Trail is all booked up, it's too expensive, or you would rather try out something different, the Salkantey Trek could be right up your street. This trek typically lasts for five days and will take you through winding passes to high altitude jungle. Some tour companies also offer part of the trek on mountain bike.

58. Discover the Pre-Hispanic Sun and Moon Temples

If you're a history buff and you can't get enough of ancient ruins, it's a mistake to think that your adventures will begin and end with Machu Picchu because this is far from the case. Just 5km south of Trujillo city, you can also find the Sun and Moon Temples, impressive structures that were built by the pre-hispanic Mochica people of Peru. Archaeologists have discovered that the Sun Temple was built in just 3 days by a staggering number of 250,000 men.

59. Munch on an Alpaca Burger in Cusco

The alpaca is an ever present animal in the city of Cusco. As well as being able to find many textiles made with alpaca wool, you can also chow down on alpaca meat at a variety of restaurants and fondas. For a burger that you won't forget in a hurry, we can heartily recommend a trip to Papacho's in Cusco, a place that serves up gourmet burgers and nothing but. You'll also be pleased to know that alpaca meat is low in calories, fat, and cholesterol, and high in protein, so it might just be the healthiest burger you'll ever eat.

60. Pass a Few Pleasant Beach Days at Mancora

When you think of beach locations around the world or in Latin America, it's very unlikely that Peru is the first spot that springs to mind, but if you can't get enough of fun in the sun, there's certainly some local beach options that you should know about. Mancora is one of our favourite beach spots in Peru. You won't find huge and overdeveloped resorts, but a quaint fishing village that has buckets of charm. Rent a bungalow on the edge of beach and enjoy the relaxed pace of life.

61. Visit an Inca Fortress in the Clouds, Kuelap

If you have an interest in the ancient civilisations of Peru, you should think way beyond Machu Picchu. We think that one of the most magical places that history lovers can visit is Kuelap, a walled city built by the Chachapoyas people in the 6th century. It is located 3000 metres above sea level in the mountains of the Andes, and with its walls of 20 metres in height, this was most likely a place of great defence. Kuelap would have once had a population of 3000 warriors, shamans, farmers, and merchants.

62. Eat Peruvian Comfort Food, Aji de Gallina

Some of the food in Peru is definitely quite adventurous for Westerners who are used to chicken breasts in supermarket packaging. If you are squeamish about eating cow's heart or guinea pig, something that might suit you better is a delicious local chicken stew called Aji de Gallina. For this dish, chicken thighs are cooked in a sweet condensed milk sauce that's thickened with nuts and breads, and it's the very definition of comfort food.

63. Discover Traditional Crafts in Ichimay Wari

When you need to go souvenir shopping, it can be a good idea to steer clear of the country's biggest cities and shopping centres. Instead, take a trip to Ichimay Wari in the Lurin district of the country. This is a collective of artisans from the Huarpas and Wari cultures who are unbelievably talented. As well as shopping for goodies, this is a place to actually try your hand at being a craftsperson. They have workshops in many things like weaving, traditional pottery, and more.

64. Visit the Peaceful Inca Site of Tambomachay

While in Cusco, Machu Picchu is not the only ancient Inca site that you can visit. If you have the bug for ancient history, you'll also want to pay a visit to an Inca site called

Tambomachay, which includes a series of waterfalls, aqueducts, and canals that run through the terraced stone ruins of the structure. It is a great monument to the skills of Andean architects who could blend buildings with the natural environment with enormous talent.

65. Tuck Into a Hearty Bowl of Pachamanca

Because the regions of Peru are very different from each other and with different climates, you can expect to find different types of food as you travel from place to place. When you find your way to the Andes, something very commonly served up is Pachamanca, a dish baked with hot stones, with either lamb, mutton, pork, chicken, or guinea pig as the star of the show. This is rustic cooking and eating at its best, and it dates way back to pre-hispanic times.

66. Be Stunned by the Church of San Francisco

Peru is a very religious country, and this means that you can find some stunning church architecture, particularly in the capital city, Lima. Without a doubt, the most impressive church of them all in Lima is the Church of San Francisco. The church has been built in the Baroque style of the late 1600s, with an incredible lattice dome. But the highlight of the church are the catacombs, and there are approximately 75,000 bodies buried underneath the church.

67. Hike the Llanganuco Lakes

If you love nothing more than to feel the clean air in your lungs on a brisk hike, Peru is the place for you, and we are not just talking about the Inca Trail. There are many other spectacular and challenging hikes, and one of our favourites has to be hiking around the picturesque Llanganunco Lakes. You can find these twin lakes in Huascaran National Park. This is a day hike that only takes around 2-5 hours, and it's doable for most people with an okay fitness level. The stunning turquoise blue of the lakes will make it well worth the effort.

68. Sip on Peruvian Wines as the Fiesta de la Vendimia

Peru may not be the most famous country in the world for wine production, but this is certainly not to say that there is no wine culture in Peru, and we can guarantee that any wine lover will have the time of their life at the Fiesta de la Vendimia, a special wine festival in Ica that celebrates the grape harvest at the beginning of March. As well as being able to taste local wines, there's a local beauty pageant, street processions, and lots of music and dancing.

69. Try a Taste of China in Peru

Peruvian food is so diverse that when you order a bowl of Sopa Rachi and it arrives at the table, you could be forgiven for thinking that you have found yourself in China. This Peruvian dish is actually very similar to Chinese congee – a Chinese savoury porridge. Sopa Rachi tends to consist of a thick rice porridge, that has toppings such as beef intestine, green onions, and bean sprouts.

70. Party With Locals at Gotica in Lima

Peru is a country best known for its culture and landscapes, but if you need to let loose now and again, you'll certainly have no problem finding places to party, particularly when you are in the capital city. For our money, Gotica is the best of all the nightclubs in Lima, and as its name would suggest, the interior is cavernous, moody, and darkly atmospheric. It's the place to be for happening electronic music, and big name DJs often play there.

71. Swim in the Pools of Catarata de Bayoz

If you love the natural world, Peru offers countless experiences. But when you don't want to be shoulder to shoulder with other tourists, which is the best place to get away from it all and really have an immersive experience in Peru's landscapes? For this, we recommend a hike through the jungle to a waterfall called Catarta de Bayoz. One of the nicest things about this place is the pools of warm water at the bottom of the falls that you'll most likely have all to yourself.

72. Sip on a Pisco Sour at Gran Hotel Bolivar

The Gran Hotel Bolivar in Lima is one of the most iconic hotels in Peru. It opened in 1924, and it has attracted famous names such as Orson Welles, John Wayne, and Ava Gardner through its doors. If you can't afford to spend the night in this fancy hotel, worry not, because you're still very welcome at the bar where the only drink you should be thinking about is the iconic Pisco Sour. This Peruvian cocktail combines pisco with key lime, egg white, sugar, ice, and bitters.

73. Explore Peru's pre-Inca Empire, the Chan Chan Ruins

While Machu Picchu is certainly the most iconic Inca site in Peru, the largest pre-Columbian city in the Americas is not Machu Picchu but the Chan Chan ruins, which can be found just outside of Trujillo. The city was built around 1300AD and covered an area of 20 square kilometres. These days, much has been washed away by flooding, but you can still see impressive broad plazas, a royal burial chamber, and a lot of intricate design work.

74. Chow Down on Ceviche From La Mar in Lima

Of course, if there is one food that's synonymous with Peru it's ceviche. Ceviche is essentially fresh fish or seafood that is cooked in the acidity of lemon or lime for a short time so that it's still tender and full of flavour. There's certainly no shortage of places to enjoy ceviche in Peru, but if you feel like going all out, we can recommend a restaurant called La Mar in Peru. This is often considered to be one of the best restaurants in Latin America, and the sea urchin ceviche is something unique and special that no foodie should miss.

75. Relax in the Hot Springs, Banos de los Novios

If you find yourself in Lima and wanting to escape the big city for a couple of days for an atmosphere that's a little more relaxed, we can recommend a trip to Churin, a town in the mountains that is around a 4 hour drive from Lima, and it's famous for its incredible hot spring complexes, of which there are three. The waters are warm and full of sulphuric content that are useful for treating rheumatic ailments and easing weary muscles.

76. Join in With the Festivities of the Marinera Festival

The local Peruvian people love to celebrate special occasions and have a good time together, and this is never more evident than at the annual Marinera Festival, which takes place in Trujillo around the middle of January each year. The Marinera is actually a local dance that originates from the coast of Peru, and the performers act out falling in love with the movement of their bodies and handkerchiefs they use as props.

77. Brush Up Your Spanish Skills

While it's true that Peru does have a well worn tourist and backpacker path, and that people in your hostels and hotels will probably speak some English, your experience will be so much richer if you can talk to people in their own language. Fortunately, Peru is positively littered with Spanish language schools that are very reasonably priced, so if you have the opportunity, be sure to sign up for a week or two of lessons before you start travelling around. We particularly like the Wiracocha Spanish School in Cusco.

78. Explore a Moche Ceremonial Complex, El Brujo

If you are interested in ruins and ancient Peru, you've probably heard that Cusco is the place to be, but actually the city of Trujillo has more accessible ruins. One of these archaeological complexes is called El Brujo, which is an ancient monument of the Moche culture. Back then, it was one of the most important religious sites for Moche culture, and it held many treasures and even stored a famous mummy, the Lady of Cao.

79. Eat the Best Sandwich of Your Life at La Lucha Sangucheria

Yes, Peruvian food is awesome, but sometimes you just want something simple to eat on the go, and that's when you head to La Lucha Sangucheria in the Miraflores district of Lima for the very best sandwich of your life. The really awesome thing about this place, other than the yumminess of it all, is that it's open really late, and one of these bursting full sandwiches makes great drunk food. We highly recommend the suckling pig.

80. Climb to the Top of El Misti

Of course, the most famous trekking route in Peru is across the Inca trail, and while this trek is certainly challenging for most people, it might not satisfy people who love to hike to the tops of mountains on a regular basis. If you really want a challenge, hiking the El Misti volcano is something you might want to do. Only five to ten people a week try to climb the slopes because it's so challenging. Would you dare?

81. Treat Yourself to Picarones, a Yummy Street Food Snack

When it's 5pm, and lunchtime has long past but it's not quite dinner time yet, something that you can put into your mouth to satisfy a peckish hunger is a street food snack called picarones. This is essentially the Peruvian version of a doughnut. The thick batter is not, however, like any kind of doughnut batter you've tasted before, as it's typically made from squash and sweet potato. The fried rings are then coated in a sweet and sticky syrup.

82. Celebrate the Festival of the Sun in Sacsayhuaman

If you want to learn about Inca culture in Peru, visiting the ruins is great but attending an ancient Inca festival is even better. The Festival of the Sun is something that takes place in Sacsayhuaman, and dates back 500 years to the Inca heyday. Ritual sacrifice used to be part of the festivities, but these days it's altogether tamer. The main event is a street procession filled with music, dancers, prayers, scattered flowers, and women sweeping away evil spirits.

83. Keep Your Kids Happy at the Ghost Train Park

Whether you are travelling with kids or you are a big kid yourself, the Ghost Train Park in Lima is an awesome place to let your playful streak run wild. This disused outdoor space has recently been revamped with recycled materials to create a fun outdoor adventure, with things like canopy lines, swings, and climbing structures. What's more, it's completely free to go there and join in with the fun.

84. Chow Down on Carapulcra, a Peruvian Pork Stew

There are endless local dishes to try in Peru, and one of the most enduringly popular that you'll find all over the country is called Carapulcra. The name might sound exotic, but actually the flavours will be quite familiar to most travellers as this is essentially a meat and potato stew. What makes the dish really special, is that it has a mix of Inca, European, and African flavours that make it really complex. In the sauce, you'll find peanuts, cloves, hot peppers, anise, cinnamon, and red wine.

85. Honour Peru's Recent History at the Place of Memory

Of course, to understand a country you have to take the time to understand its history. But while much emphasis has been placed upon Peru's ancient history, the last century has not been easy on the country either, and between 1980 and 2000, 70,000 people died in fights between government forces and insurgent groups. You can find the Place of Memory in Lima, a place to honour recent history so as not to repeat it.

86. Say Hi to Monkeys at La Isla de Los Monos

If the idea of totally immersing yourself in the incredible landscapes of Peru sounds appealing to you, you should know about La Isla de Los Monos, or Monkey Island. As the name would suggest, this place is monkey central. There are eight species of monkeys that live on the island, and they're all so abundant that it's certainly not out of the question to see them all. The monkeys are mostly mischievous but not dangerous, and being totally surrounded by them at all times is quite the "back to nature" experience.

87. Admire the Art Deco Architecture Along Jiron de la Union

We think that one of the best ways to understand a new city is to simply walk around, and Lima is a very beautiful city for walking. One of the most enduringly popular walking streets is called Jiron de la Union, which can be found in the city's historic centre. The street was built in 1535, the same year Peru was founded, but has changed immensely since then. You can now find stunning neoclassical and art deco buildings along the street.

88. Keep Warm With Alpaca Scarves and Sweaters

As you travel around Peru, you will no doubt notice some differences in the climate, and one of the chilliest parts has to be Cusco because of its altitude. Fortunately, it's really not too difficult to wrap up and keep warm considering the amount of Alpaca wool products you will find all around you. Purchasing an Alpaca scarf or sweater is a great way of keeping the warmth in, and it also makes a fantastic souvenir to take home.

89. Try a Plate of Chanfainita

When the Spanish people brought African slaves to Peru, the slaves could not afford to eat regular cuts of meat and were limited to the entrails. Thanks to their influence, this is now a major part of Peruvian cuisine, and it's never shown off more deliciously than in Chanfainita. The main ingredient of this dish is cows' lungs, which are cooked with onion, potato, and some spices, and then served up in a meaty broth. This is meaty, hearty, and totally delicious.

90. Look Out Over Lima From Cerro San Cristobal

Cerro San Cristobal is a hill on the outskirts of Lima city, and from the top you can take in some of the most spectacular views of the imaginable. This hill is quite the climb, but fear not because there are also local buses that can pretty much take you to the top. It's a good idea to set off early so that you can get to the top of the hill before the clouds arrive.

91. Spend a Romantic Day in the Parque del Amor

If you are travelling to Peru with your partner, and you are looking forward to some alone time together, there is nowhere quite as romantic as the Parque del Amor, a park that is situated in the beautiful Miraflores district of Lima. This park is located on cliffs that overlook the Pacific Ocean, and it's surrounded by walls of mosaic tiles and romantic quotes. There is also an incredible statue of a couple embraced in a kiss in the park.

92. Go Mountain Biking Along the Colca Canyon

For outdoorsy types in Peru, there is almost endless amounts of explore, and we think that the Colca Canyon is a very special and yet overlooked place in the country. The Colca Canyon, located in the south of the country, is almost twice as deep as the Grand Canyon. This is popular territory for trekkers, but even more so with adventurous mountain bikers. There are a couple of tour companies nearby that can provide everything you need to have an unforgettable biking experience in the canyon.

93. Rock Out for Rock En La Playa

When you think of places to visit for rock music festivals, it's very unlikely that Peru is the first country that will cross your mind. But if you are a massive rock fan, you'll be pleased to know that Peru has its very own rock festival called Rock En La Playa. Don't expect any big name international bands, but if you fancy rocking out on the beach to Peruvian music, this could be up your alley.

94. Have a Sandboarding Adventure in Huacachina

Adventure travellers are attracted to Peru for one major reason: the Inca Trail. But if you are not such a keen hiker, fear not because there are tonnes of other adventures that you can try out, and one of the coolest of these is sandboarding on the sand dunes of Haucachina, a village in the southwest of the country. If you have tried snowboarding before, this is very similar but with sand instead of snow!

95. Fill Your Stomach at Mistura Food Festival

Peruvian food is well known for being as diverse as it is delicious, and what better way to experience all the deliciousness of Peruvian grub than by attending a local food festival? This is exactly what you can do in Lima at the beginning of September for the Mistura Food Festival. Around 350 producers from all over the world are invited to showcase their wares, including 50 restaurants, 70 food trucks, and lots more culinary goodness besides.

96. Take a Sea Kayaking Tour From Lima

Something very special about Lima is that as well as being a cultural capital city, it's also a coastal city so you get to experience a sea breeze and even have some adventures out on the open water. Something that all ages can enjoy is a spot of gentle sea kayaking. You will be guided out on to the water by professionals while you take in the city skyline. And if you are lucky, you might even see dolphins or sealions in the water.

97. Visit the Pisac Sunday Market

If you find yourself in Cusco on a Sunday and you aren't sure what to do with your time, one thing you can do is pay a day trip to Pisac, a small town that is just 35km outside of Cusco. This is a market town through and through, and while the market is open every day of the week, it is truly magnificent on Sundays when it explodes in size. The artisan market is a great place to purchase cool souvenirs – just be prepared to bargain hard on the price.

98. Enjoy Slatherings of Coca Marmalade on Toast in Cusco

If you have not heard of the coca plant before, it might ring a bell when you are told that it's the coca leaf that is used to produce cocaine. It is illegal virtually everywhere in the world even to consume it as coca, but not in Cusco where it is often used to help people acclimatise to the city's high altitude. One of the most unique transformations of coca in Cusco is for it to be turned into a thick marmalade, which you can spread on your toast in the morning time.

99. Discover Ancient Artefacts at the National Museum of Archaeology

Peru is a country with an incredible expanse of history, and you can get right up close to Peru as it was thousands of years ago in the National Museum of Archaeology in Lima. This is the most important history museum in Peru, with exhibits pertaining to pre-Columbian, colonial, and republican Peru. Some of the more interesting artefacts are the elongated skulls from 2000 years ago in Paracas.

100. Go Textiles Shopping in Cusco

There is an incredible weaving tradition in the mountains of Peru, and in Cusco you'll find countless places to purchase some great textiles. But how are you to know which are really the best and most authentic places to make your purchase? Well, we think that the Centro de Textiles Tradicionales de Cusco is a very special place indeed. This shop supports a 10,000 year old tradition, and everything on sale there is hand made.

101. Start Your Day with a Coffee From BuenaVista Café

If you are the kind of person who can't start their day without a strong caffeine boost, you shouldn't have too much trouble finding good coffee in Peru. But if you're in Lima and don't know where to start your coffee search, trust us when we sat that BuenaVista Café is the place to be. The coffee is fantastic, but equally impressive is the view, and you are able to sit on their terrace and watch the waves lap up against the shore as you sip on your morning latte.

Before You Go…

Thanks for reading **101 Coolest Things to Do in Peru**. We hope that it makes your trip a memorable one!

Keep your eyes peeled on **www.101coolestthings.com**, and have an incredible time in Peru.

Team 101 Coolest Things

18999543R00031

Printed in Great Britain
by Amazon